CAMPING GAMES

for

Adult

couples & groups

Contents

Introduction

There was once a time when I considered myself un-outdoorsy. I was the chubby kid at school who came last in sports field runs (....and I don't mean that as a figure of speech. I once did a school run with 200 of my classmates, and I came in last place!)

So how does the kid from school who detested sports go on to have possibly the coolest job in the world.....a professional adventurer?!

Really, it all began with a walk. A big walk!

In my mid-twenties, I found myself recently married, living in London and doing all the things city people do.

I had a 9-5 desk-based job. Long commutes to and from work. Most of my money went on paying rent on our tiny, mouldy loft-floor studio flat. And all my energies went into making it to the weekend when I'd let my hair down with friends over a few too many overpriced drinks.

In time, my unhealthy lifestyle began to take a toll on my mental health, and I was feeling ground down with the slog of trying to find work that I enjoyed. I'd tried all sorts of jobs. From a personal assistant, a charity fundraiser and a secondary school teacher. But none of them suited me.

Then, one day, while on my lunch break at work, an article from National Geographic caught my eye while scrolling on Facebook: 'World's Best Hikes: Epic Trails'

There, I saw the Israel National Trail listed - a 1000km trek the length of Israel, including a crossing of the vast Negev desert. I was instantly drawn to the idea of being in the vast open desert (it may have been the January cold!).

I'd never even been aware that there were such things as long-distance trails. Suddenly, I was stuck down a Google rabbit hole reading loads of blogs by cool people going on adventures.

In a moment, I decided on a whim that I wanted to do this hike, and later that day, I managed to convince my husband to join me.

Over the next year, we sold most of our possessions, went on a few courses to learn about navigation and wild camping, handed in our notices at work and on our flat...... and boarded a plane....

* * *

BUILDING A DREAM LIFE OF ADVENTURE

The hike was one of the most incredible experiences of my life!

The trail completely changed me and the trajectory of my life. I built back my confidence and self-esteem and discovered a deep-rooted passion for all things adventure and the outdoors.

I was also determined to start pursuing work that I actually wanted to do. The sort of work that made me feel excited to get up in the morning.

While on the hike, I kept up a blog (www.bexband.com), which had started gaining traction. I loved writing, sharing my adventures, and inspiring others, so I began doing sponsored posts and delivering talks.

I also launched a women's adventure community called Love Her Wild (www.loveherwild.com).

The idea came about because I'd not met a single woman hiking the trail. I wanted to encourage more women to get outdoors, taking on challenges to start realising their full potential while also reconnecting to nature.

I gained an outdoor leader qualification and started organising and taking women on epic adventures.

When I launched the community and my blog, I never imagined how successful they would become!

Love Her Wild now has tens of thousands of members. My blog has had millions of readers. I'm a bestselling, award-winning author. And (the best part) I get to live a life full of adventure and get paid for doing what I love most.

* * *

GAMES & THE OUTDOORS

Of all the adventures I'm lucky to go on, there is nothing in my mind that beats the simple act of camping out under the stars, especially with friends and family in tow. I do it as often as I can.

I've gained a bit of a reputation as being the 'games' person. I always have a game or activity up my sleeve to help bring some laughter and fun to any camping situation.

When friends kept asking me for game ideas, I had the idea for this book! It's a compilation of all the camping games, activities and prompts I've collected over the years from all over the world.

I hope it brings you many hours of fun!

So flick through the book and find a page that takes your fancy. Grab some friends or a partner, and let the play begin......

* * *

Don't forget to give me a follow for more inspiration and advice on all things outdoors and adventure:

IG & FB: @Bex_Band

YouTube: @BandFamilyAdventures

Newsletter: www.bexband.com/sign-up/

GAMES FOR GROUPS

Can you Hear me?

I can't play this game without ending up in fits of laughter. It's both ridiculous and genius! It gets noisy, so you'll want to be somewhere you won't disturb others.

Number of players: minimum 3, maximum 8
Equipment needed: none
Style of game: mildly active

• Get into teams of two. Pick a team to play first and have players stand facing each other, roughly 20 meters apart (as you play more rounds, you can make it harder by increasing the distance). They are the Shouter and the Hearer. In between the Shouter and the Hearer, the other players congregate.
• The Shouter picks a phrase, ie, 'Going for a walk in the woods'.
• The Hearer will count down from 3 and then shout 'Go'. At this point, the Shouter needs to shout the phrase. They can move sideways and use actions and gestures, but can't step any closer.

• On 'Go,' the rest of the players will try their best to drown out the sound of the Shouter (making any kind of noise they want) and block their view so the hearer can't lip-read or see the gestures.

• The Shouter can say the phrase up to 4 times, after which the round stops and the Hearer has to guess what the phrase was.

• The team get a point if they get it right. Switch teams and keep track of points to see who wins.

Campfire Psychiatrists

Psychiatrists is a great game to kick off your evening. It's funny and a good conversation starter. However, you can only play it once, as once you know the game, you can 'act' but can't be a Guesser.

Note that your guessers will need to be able to see the players, so you'll need good light. This game also only works if everyone knows each other fairly well.

Number of Players: minimum 3, maximum 16
Equipment needed: none
Style of game: sitting

- Pick 3 - 6 players who know the game to be your actors. The actors sit next to each other, facing the rest of the players, who are the Guessers.
- The game is for the Guessers to work out what 'condition' the players have.
- The actors 'condition' is that they have adopted the personality of the person to their right (the person sitting on the far left adopts the personality of the person first in line).

• Guessers can ask any one of the players a question - any question they can think of - and the player must respond how they think the person to their right would answer.

• If they answer correctly, then nothing is said, and they continue to the next question.

• If they get it wrong, then the person they are supposed to be imitating shouts 'switch' and the players swap places randomly, now adopting the new person who is on the right.

• This game will initially confuse the Guessers, but as it goes on, they will get closer to working it out. If they are really stuck, you can recommend asking the same question to the same person, as they will have a different answer after switching.

• When a Guesser thinks they know the answer, rather than shouting it out, they must whisper it to one of the actors who will say if they are right or not.

• If a Guesser gets it right, they then join the actors and adopt the same 'condition'. This creates even more confusion!

• Keep going until everyone has worked it out.

Campsite Ghost-Hunt

A good game to whip out at the end of the night after a few beers. The darker it is outside, the more fun the game is.

Number of players: minimum 6, no maximum
Equipment needed: 2 sleeping bags and 2 team bases
Style of game: mildly active

- Divide into two teams, each with a tent (or another hidden space) as their designated base. Teams retreat into their tents, where a member is secretly chosen to become a Campsite Ghost. They do this by putting a sleeping bag over themselves (standing up) so they are no longer identifiable (they might need to take off shoes)
- The Campsite Ghost from each team emerges. Their goal is to determine the identity of the other team's ghost while remaining hidden themselves; by poking, feeling or making them laugh, but can't pull the sleeping bag off.
- The ghosts only get one guess. If a Campsite Ghost guesses wrong, the watching teammates shout 'wrong,' and the other player now gets a guess. If both get it wrong, neither player wins, and you play another round.
- If the other ghost is correctly identified, the guessed person will join the correct guessers team.
- The game ends when one team recruits every member from the opposing team. When a team loses, just one person will be left.

WATER THROW

Play this on a hot day when the thought of getting wet sounds quite appealing!

Number of players: minimum 2, no maximum
Equipment needed: water balloons (I suggest eco reusable water balloons)
Style of game: mildly active

• Pair off. Pairs face each other a few metres apart, one with a filled water balloon in hand.
• When the game starts, the players with the water balloons throw the balloons to their teammates. When they catch it successfully, both players take a small step backwards.
• The game continues this way until the water balloon bursts, at which point the team are out of the game.
• The winning team are the one that can get the furthest distance apart from each other without the water balloon bursting.

HEAD-TORCH
Sweep

Head-Torch Sweep is a quick and easy game to play. A good location is key, as you need lots of obstacles. A forest is ideal. A campsite can work, but you may want to add some additional fun hiding options, such as sleeping bags and chairs.

Number of players: minimum 4, no maximum
Equipment needed: a strong head-torch or torch
Style of game: mildly active

- Decide on a spot at one end of your allocated playing space where your Catcher will stand. And a point, at the other end of the space, where all your Hiders are going to start.
- The Catcher puts the flashlight or head-torch on full beam and either holds it rigid at waist length or has it secured to their head.
- The Catcher starts the game by shouting 'go' and starts to rotate in a continual circle on the spot (like a lighthouse). After 'go' all hiders quickly run to find their first hiding spot..

• The aim of the game is for the Hiders to tap the Catcher on the shoulder without being caught. If any part of the Hider is on view when the light from the Catcher next comes around - and the Catcher can identify who the person is - then they are out of the game.

• The Hiders have until the Catcher does another full circle (and the light reaches them again) to move and find a new hiding space.

• The Catcher should start by turning slowly, but can speed up as the game goes on to make it harder.

• The first player to tap the Catcher on the shoulder wins and will be the Catcher in the next round.

TENTS & PEGS

Tents and Pegs is a take on a classic summer camp game. It's a high-energy and fun running-around game. It also gets very competitive, so watch out for cheating! You'll need a large-ish grassy area to play.

Number of players: minimum 10, no maximum
Equipment needed: 12 bits of 'treasure' (could use plastic cups, balls or even rocks)
Style of game: Active

- Mark out your playing space, which should be a large, flat area. At each end of the area, a line is marked out (either by cones or another sort of indicator such as jumpers) - these are the bases for the opposing teams.
- You'll also need to mark out a centre line - halfway between the two prisons - in the same way.
- In each base lay out 6 treasure pieces, Make sure they are spread out evenly.
- Each team has one-half of the field, and they attack toward their opponents ' base.
- The leader signals when the game has begun. The goal of the players is to cross their opponents area to reach their base a retrieve a piece of treasure.
- As soon as a player crosses the centre line, they may be tagged and thus made prisoners.

• Prisoners are escorted by the person who caught them to the captor's base. Prisoners must go quietly and captors may only tag again once they have led the prisoner back to their prison. They are then free to continue playing.
• Any player who makes it past their opponent's base line is safe from being tagged. They can then choose to either take one piece of treasure back to their own base or release one prisoner by tagging. Whatever they decide to pick, they must bring back to their own base (walking outside of the play area). Once back in their own base, they (and the prisoner they've freed, if that's who they picked) can then continue playing again.
• The game is won when one team has all twelve pieces of treasure in play on their base line.
• If the game finishes too quickly, you can increase the number of treasure or make the play area wider to make it more of a challenge.

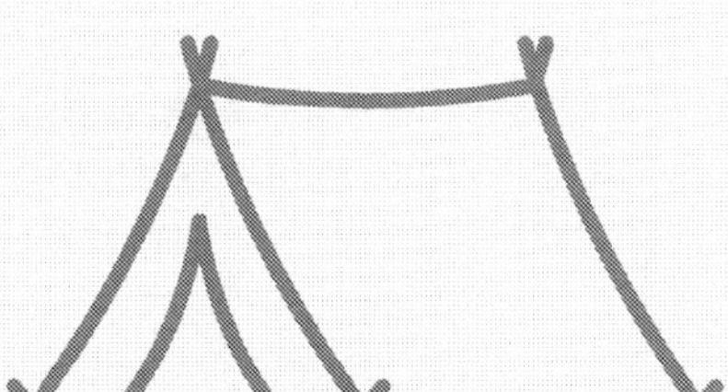

NARCISSISTS

It takes a bit of time to set up this game up, but it's well worth the effort. Part of the fun with this game is everyone being suspicious of each other!

Number of players: minimum 5, no maximum
Equipment needed: none
Style of game: mildly active

:

•There will need to be an appointed leader to organise and run the game. This is best played when you are with the same people over a period of time (no players can leave or join once started).

• In secret, the leader writes everybody's name down on a list at random. The player's task is to 'kill' the person whose name is underneath theirs (the person at the end of the list has to kill the first person).

• They do this by tricking that person into doing an act: this could be acting like a dog, giving them a piggyback, wearing an item of someone else's clothing, singing a song, standing on one leg, etc. It has to be a task that is manageable but not too easy.

• The Leader gives everyone a piece of paper with the name of the person they have to 'kill' and the task they have to get them to do to 'kill' them. This must be kept top secret.

• If that person succeeds in getting their person killed, they can reveal this to the person straight away and then tells the leader who crosses that person off the list - they are out of the competition. The person who has just been killed must hand over their piece of paper with their person and task: the killer now takes on their task.

• In the end, there will be just one winner...the name of the game is that they may have 'killed' 10 people or just 1, and it was that person who did all the hard work to get people to carry out tasks.

• This is a fun game with many tactics, as it becomes very difficult to get people to do a task willingly when everyone gets suspicious!

CAMPERS COUNT

This is a ridiculously simple game, which sounds like it wouldn't be much fun, but in actual fact, it's surprisingly difficult and quickly addictive.

Number of players: *minimum 5, maximum 15*
Equipment needed: *none*
Style of game: *sitting*

- *Players lie or sit with their eyes closed.*
- *Start by trying to reach the number 10 as a team. You can then make the next round harder by making it 15.*
- *Without instruction, a player can start the game off at any time by saying 'one'.*
- *Another player (any player) can choose to then say 'two'. And then another will say 'three'. And so on.*
- *A player can say more than one number, but not in a row.*
- *If players both say the number at the same time, then the game is lost and you must start again.*

Gutter Tent CHALLENGE

This is a team game. If you want to make it competitive, you can split everyone into 2 teams and have them race each other.

Number of players: minimum 2, maximum 10
Equipment needed: plastic gutters (one for each person), a tennis ball
Style of game: mildly active

•• Each player is given a plastic gutter.
• The game starts in a tent, where there will be one player (or one player from each team if you are competing) who has a plastic gutter and a tennis ball.
• That player balances the ball on their gutter and then shouts 'Go', at which point the game starts.
• The team/s must get the tennis ball out of the tent and into a different tent (choose a tent far enough away to make the challenge interesting enough).
• When a teammate has the tennis ball in their gutter, they can not move their legs, cannot touch the ball, and the ball cannot fall to the ground. If any of these things happen, the team have to start again.
• If playing against teams, the first one to get their ball to the last tent wins.
• If you are playing as one team, time yourself and then see if you can beat your time on the next try.

EARTH, AIR WATER!

This is a great little game that tests memory and quick thinking.

Number of players: minimum 5, maximum 20
Equipment needed: tennis ball
Style of game: sitting

• Players sit/stand in a circle. The Leader is in the middle with a ball.
• Just before the leader throws the ball at a chosen player, they say either "Earth", "Air", or "Water". The player must catch the ball and name a creature that inhabits the environment.
• If the player hesitates for more than a second, they are out.
• No creature may be named more than once: if a player names a creature already used, they are out.
• The player is also out if they drop the ball (as long as it was a fair throw).
• The last player standing wins.

Dragons

This is a fun game to play with a competitive group. To make it fair, mix up the teams so they have a range of heights and abilities.

Number of players: minimum 6, no maximum
Equipment needed: none
Style of game: active

• Two teams line up, one person behind the other. Everyone puts both hands on the shoulder of the player in front. The two teams are the 'dragons'.
• The front players of each dragon are blindfolded and guided by the players behind, either by tapping their shoulders to get them to move left or right, or by having the team shout instructions (you can play two rounds, one with each variation).
• The ultimate challenge is for each dragon to guide their blindfolded player to touch the rearmost member of the opposing dragon, scoring a point for their team.
• The dragons must maintain their hold on each other's shoulders at all times.

BLINDFOLDED SHOE SHUFFLE

A daft game that will bring lots of laughs. This is just as fun for the person who sits out of the game to shuffle the shoes!

Number of players: minimum 3, maximum 10
Equipment needed: none
Style of game: mildly active

- Each person takes off their shoes and throws them into the middle of the circle. They then put on a blindfold or close their eyes if they can be trusted.
- Someone who is not playing then shuffles up the shoes.
- On 'go', the blind players must attempt to find their shoes and put them on.
- The first to do this successfully wins.
- You can add in other items to this game to make it harder, such as a jumper or headtorch for each player.

Pterodactyl is a game guaranteed to have you all laughing. You'll need to be able to see each other, so it's best played in the day or early evening.

Number of players: *minimum 5, maximum 15*
Equipment needed: *none*
Style of game: *sitting*

- *Players sit in a circle so they can all see each other.*
- *When starting the game, the first player turns to the player on their left and says 'pterodactyl' without showing their teeth, i.e. their lips need to be over their teeth as if impersonating someone who has lost their teeth.*
- *This continues clockwise until someone decides to switch direction by turning back to the person who just said 'pterodactyl' and letting out a screech like a dinosaur (keep those teeth covered!)*
- *The person receiving the screech has two options: they can continue in this new direction by saying 'pterodactyl' to the person on their right, or they can reverse the direction again by screeching back at the previous player.*
- *If a player shows their teeth at any time (it's hard not to when you're laughing!), then they are out.*

Pterodactyl

Beanie Hat

Beanie Hat is similar to charades but with more challenges. It's fun to play in competing teams, but you can also play as a single group if you don't have enough players.

Number of players: minimum 4, maximum 20
Equipment needed: pen and paper
Style of game: active

• Each player receives around 3-5 slips of paper.. They write a phrase on each slip (you can choose a theme in advance, such as films or books).
• Slips are folded and all tossed into a beanie hat. Players are split into two teams.
• For the first round, a player from the first team is given 1 minute. They pick a slip of paper from the bowl and have to use verbal clues to describe what's on the paper to their team without using any of the words on the paper (charades, but in spoken form). Once their team guesses correctly, they pick up a new slip, doing as many as possible until the time runs out.

• Now, a player from the other team stands up and has one minute to do the same.
• Keep going, switching players, until all the slips are used up. Put them back in the beanie hat.
• Now, play a second round; this time, players can't use words and can only use gestures (like charades).
• Then play a final round, but this time, players are only allowed to say a one-word clue (a word that doesn't appear on the slip).
• Each correct guess is a point. Keep track of points - the team with the most at the end wins.

Bombing

This is a good one to play when you want to get active and run around for a bit.

Number of players: minimum 8, no maximum
Equipment needed: ball
Style of game: active

- A square is marked out, and all the players stand inside this square, except for 2 "on" players who stand outside the square, with one on each side.
- The two players 'on' throw a ball at those in the square, passing it among themselves if they wish.
- Any player who is hit must join the throwers outside of the square, and they also become 'on'.
- Hits must be hit below the waist to count.
- The last player remaining in the square is the winner and chooses someone to join them as a bomber in the next game.

Heads or Tails

This is a good little filler game you can play before kicking off a new game or activity. I often play Heads and Tails if I ever need to select someone, such as the person who will be first 'on' for a new game. Or you can use it as a forfeit - the last person standing has to do all the washing up, etc!

Number of players: minimum 4, no maximum
Equipment needed: a coin
Style of game: sitting

- All players need to stand up.
- One person will be running the game. That person needs a coin in their hand, which they throw up in the air and slap down on the back of their hand.
- Before revealing the coin, they will say, 'Heads or tails.' At this point, all the players will need to pick either 'heads' by putting both hands on their heads or 'tails' by putting both hands on their bum.
- The caller reveals whether the coin is heads-up (the heads win) or tails-up (the tails win). The losing members sit down.
- Make sure that not everyone has chosen the same for each round; otherwise, there will be no winners and losers.
- Continue until just one player is left - your winner (or the person who gets a forfeit).

WEREWOLVES

Have you ever seen the TV series Traitors? This is the original game that inspired the series, and it's just as addictive to play. It takes a little time to get familiar with the pacing of the rounds. But once cracked, I guarantee this will become a firm favourite on all your camping trips!

Number of players: minimum 9, maximum 20
Equipment needed: none
Style of game: sitting

- In this game, one person assumes the role of the leader (they control the game but don't play, so you'll want to switch this person around if you play more rounds).
- With everyone's eyes closed, the leader touches two people's heads, designating them as Werewolves.
- The Werewolves are instructed to open their eyes to identify each other and then close their eyes again.
- The leader then selects an additional person as the informant, who opens their eyes. The Werewolves raise their hands (quietly), signalling to the informant without revealing their identities.
- The rest of the participants are Villagers.

• While everyone's eyes are closed, the Werewolves open their eyes again and secretly choose a Villager to be "murdered" by quietly pointing to who they'd like to murder. At the same time, all the villages remain eyes closed.

• The leader then instructs everyone to open their eyes before announcing the murder victim.

• The Villagers must then discuss and deduce the Werewolves' identities.

• The informant can offer assistance without directly revealing names, aiming not to disclose their role (as otherwise, the Werewolves will be quick to murder them next!).

• Once the Villagers make a decision by going around the circle and doing a vote, naming the person they want to banish, the chosen person either confirms being a werewolf or reveals they inadvertently killed a fellow villager. Once murdered or banished, you are out of the game but get the joy of watching on.

• The cycle continues as everyone closes their eyes, allowing the Werewolves to select another target.

• The game concludes when both Werewolves are eliminated, in which case the Villagers have won.

• Or there's one or more Werewolves left at the end, meaning they have won.

FRENCH CRICKET

French Cricket is one of those games that, once everyone knows the rules, will be played organically throughout your camping trip. You don't need much space to play, making it a suitable game even for a busy campground.

Number of players: minimum 4, maximum 20
Equipment needed: bat (cricket bat is ideal) and a tennis ball
Style of game: Middle active

- All players form a rough, large circle around the chosen player, who stands in the middle with a cricket bat.
- The player in the middle must put their feet together and are not allowed to move once they've decided on their position.
- The chosen player must defend their legs from the oncoming ball using only the cricket bat - the rest of the players are trying to get them out by getting the tennis ball to touch their legs.
- Players can only throw the tennis ball underhand (so as not to hurt the person who is on!). They can move around, but can't move if they are holding the tennis ball. They can throw the ball between themselves to try to catch them out.

• Ensure the players in the circle aren't standing too close to give the person in the middle a chance to defend themselves.

• If someone successfully manages to get the chosen player out (by throwing the tennis ball and it touching their legs), then they are next to be on.

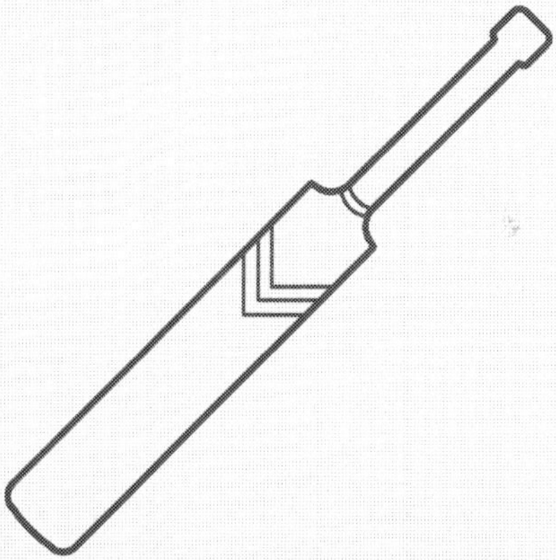

This isn't a game as such, but a fun way to trick one of your friends. You'll only be able to play the prank once, as anyone watching will know the trick. So, choose your victim wisely!

Number of players: minimum 5, maximum 20
Equipment needed: 2 sleeping bags, a tent peg
Style of game: mildly active

• 2 players hide under sleeping bags on the ground, head to toe. The rest of the players are Tappers, who stand in a circle around the players on the floor.
• A tent peg is passed around, and people can poke the players under the sleeping bags.
• When they feel a poke, the player must whip off the sleeping bag to try to see who it is - at the same time, all the Tappers quickly put their hands behind their back, concealing who did the poking.
• At some point in the game, the tent peg is passed in secret to one of the players under the sleeping bag (the one who is not being pranked), and they begin doing the poking. The player who is being pranked will start to get really frustrated that they can't work out who is doing the poking.
• Tip: to keep the game realistic, the player under the sleeping bag who now has the tent peg should pretend they have been poked once in a while and play accordingly.

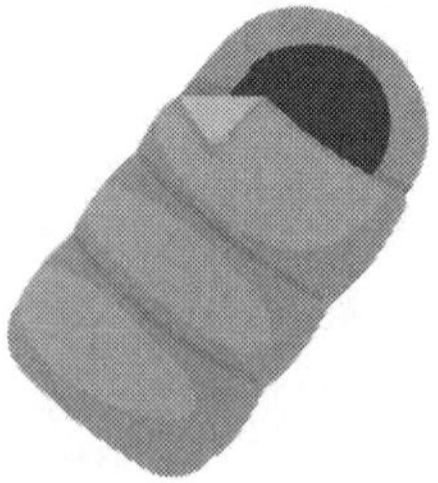

Sleeping Bag Beats

WORD ACT

Because there is some acting involved, Word Act is a nice game to play once everyone is relaxed and feeling comfortable with each other.

Number of players: minimum 5, maximum 20
Equipment needed: nothing
Style of game: sitting

- 1 or 2 people are chosen to be Guessers and move away so they are out of earshot. The remaining group decides on a word with as many letters as members in their group (i.e. if there are 5 players remaining, then a word like BRAIN or TREAT could work).
- Each person is allocated a letter from the chosen word and sits in order so they spell out the word correctly.
- Each player decides on a mood or emotion that begins with the letter that they have been allocated.
- When the Guessers return, the remaining players must be in character.
- The Guessers can ask the players questions about themselves and their likes, and the players need to answer while acting out their mood or emotion.
- The game is played until all the Guessers correctly guess the word.

SARDINES

Another one of my top games is Sardines. It always brings a lot of laughs (especially if you choose to jump out and scare people just to be mean) and stories re-told for years to come. The game has to be played in the dark - the darker the better!

Number of players: minimum 5, maximum 20
Equipment needed: nothing
Style of game: mildly active

- Before the game, you need to decipher a base (a tent is an idea) and a designated area of play. This is important as you'll be playing in the dark, so the Players need to know the boundaries. Make sure there is nothing dangerous in the play area.
- One player is chosen to be the Hider. The rest of the players stay in the base, where they can't see.
- The Hider heads out into the dark (with a flashlight, but remember to turn the flashlight off once hidden) and hides somewhere within the allocated space.
- After 2 minutes have passed, the rest of the players head out into the dark, one at a time at 1-minute intervals, to try and find the Hider.
- If they find the Hider, they join them quietly (if there are other players nearby, then wait until they are gone so you don't give the hiding place away).
- The game gets easier as more people hide. You can end up with 10 people all trying to squeeze into one hiding place!
- The game finishes when the last person finds the group - that person is the new Hider.

THROW IT AND RUN

Throw it and Run is a fun, active game. As players need to decide in each round if they should save themselves or their friends, it can stir up some pretty fun competition. You'll need a decent-sized field to play the game.

Number of players: minimum 8, no maximum
Equipment needed: tennis ball
Style of game: active

- A circle of cones or other markers is laid out: one player, who is 'it', goes in the middle, and the rest stand around the edge.
- 'It' throws a tennis ball as far as they can. Once the tennis ball has been thrown, all players start to run - the person on 'it' starts to run after the players.
- 'It' tries to tag as many of the other players as possible before one of them can reach the tennis ball, pick it up and shout 'Stop!'.
- Any player tagged stands still, then joins 'it' in the middle for the next throw.
- Only the original 'it' may throw the ball, but all players in the middle may tag once it has been thrown.
- Players round the edge at each go and may decide to save themselves or reach the tennis ball and save their friends.

Empire

Empire is equally good to play with a group that knows each other really well (as it can reveal all sorts of secrets) or with a group that doesn't know each other that well (as it gets you more familiar with each other and provides good conversation starters).
Give your players some time before you start the game to think about their secret. People struggle to think of something quickly, and if given time, they can conjure something a bit more interesting.

Number of players: minimum 8, maximum 20
Equipment needed: pen and paper
Style of game: sitting

- One person plays judge and, after calling everyone aside individually to have a chat in private, will secretly write down an interesting fact or secret from each of the players.
- In addition, they will also make up 3 fake facts.
- The judge then read all of the facts, including the made-up ones, twice to the group.

- Taking it in turns, everyone has to choose one of the facts and guess who they think it belongs to.
- If they get it right, the person the correct fact concerns is out of the game as an individual and instead joins that person's empire. The player who guessed correctly gets another go, but this time, he gets to consult with any ‘won’ players who are in their empire.
- If they guess wrong, the next person in the circle has a turn.
- If you guess somebody has an empire (i.e., they have already won people), then you win them and all of the people in their empire.
- The game ends when someone has won everybody.

The most important thing about the game is that everyone knows each other well enough to recall their names and to know what they talk like. If you are a fairly new group, wait until the end of your camping trip to play this when you all know each other a bit better.

Number of players: minimum 5, maximum 15
Equipment needed: something to act as a blindfold
Style of game: mildly active

- One person is blindfolded and positioned in the middle of the players.
- When the game begins, the group walks around the blindfolded person in a circle (or, if you prefer, have someone spin the blindfolded player until they're disoriented).
- The blindfolded player yells, 'Stop', and everyone freezes (or they are halted by the designated 'spinner').
- The blindfolded player points to someone (if they aren't directly pointing at someone, then the play will go to the nearest player) and says the name of an animal.
- The selected person must then imitate the sound of that animal, but in such a way that it isn't obvious who is making the noise. The blindfolded player can ask them to repeat the sound up to 3 times.
- If the blindfolded person correctly guesses who made the noise, they switch places; otherwise, the game continues.

Animal Noises

This game is best played as an ongoing activity over an evening or a weekend camping trip.

Number of players: minimum 3, maximum 10
Equipment needed: nothing
Style of game: sitting

- Each player selects the name of a camping item or bit of kit for themselves. For example, tent, lighter, roll mat, etc.
- The 'on' player must successfully say another player's chosen item three times (e.g., 'tent, tent, tent') before the target can say it just once.
- If they successfully say it 3 times in a row before the targeted person says it once, then that player becomes the new person 'on'. Otherwise, the original player remains in play and needs to try again.
- After a couple of rounds, everyone will realise that those with longer syllables pose a greater challenge, so you might want to give everyone a chance to switch their chosen item at some point.

CAMPING, CAMPING, CAMPING

DUTCH AUCTION

One of the great things about Dutch Auction is that there isn't a lot of skill involved - it's more about thinking, creativity, and getting in the competitive spirit of things. Someone will need to sit out of the game to lead it.

Number of players: minimum 9, maximum 15
Equipment needed: a pillowcase for each team
Style of game: mildly active

• Put everyone in teams of 3-8 players. You can have as many teams as you like competing.
• Each team is given a set amount of time to fill a pillow with random objects that they have bought with them or that they can find around the campsite. Everything must fit in the pillow case and can't stick out.
• Everyone gathers in a space with their teams, and the person leading needs to be in the middle with 3 chairs positioned back to back labelled 1st, 2nd, 3rd (you'll want to rotate the chairs during the game to keep it fair)
• The items must be kept in the pillowcases at all times unless they are being used. The leader will ask for something, such as "something to make me look pretty," "something to keep me warm," or "something useful when sleeping." Each team will rummage through their items and choose something that may fit the desired object.

• With their object in hand, the player will race to sit in the first position; if that is taken, they will aim for the second and third positions.

• They then have to explain why their item fits the description—imagination is encouraged! If the judge is happy with the description, then the team gets points (3 for first place, 2 for second and 1 point for third). If not, they must return to their team, and a new team can take their seat.

• For the last round, say, "I want something to put my pillow in!"

• Count the scores at the end of the game to see who is the winner.

• I like to mix this game up by including a few challenges after every few rounds. There could be a throwing competition using a chosen item, such as who can build the tallest tower, or a fashion contest using the items in their pillowcase.

Who Am I?

A timely classic which works well as a chilled game around the campfire.

Number of players: minimum 4, maximum 16
Equipment needed: post-it notes
Style of game: sitting

- Everyone faces each other with a post-it note on their forehead with the name of someone famous or an object (decide which in advance).
- The player to their right has decided what the person or object will be in advance and has written on the post-it and attached it to their forehead (in a way that they won't see what's written).
- Go around the circle, each player taking turns to guess what is written on their post-it note with as few questions as possible. The questions they ask can only be 'yes' or 'no' questions.
- The game continues until all players successfully identify their assigned person or object.

Hawk

A French variant of British Bulldog, but it has a little more scope for tactics as well as brute force.

Number of players: minimum 10, no maximum
Equipment needed: none
Style of game: active

• One player is chosen to be the 'hawk', and the remaining players line up at one end of the area as the 'deer'.
• When the hawk is ready, the deer tries to run from one end of the playing area to the other without being touched by the hawk. Those touched join with the hawk and, as 'wings', help to bring the deer in - but it is only the touch of the hawk that counts.
• If they wish, the wings can be split off and operate singly, in pairs or any combination, but they may not use their arms to hold the deer.
• The last 'Deer' to be caught becomes the hawk.

Leggoals is fast to set up and explain, and can be played anywhere. It's my go-to choice if I fancy something a bit active that doesn't involve running around a lot.

Number of players: minimum 6, maximum 15
Equipment needed: ball
Style of game: mildly active

- Players stand in a circle, feet fairly wide apart. Their feet must touch the neighbour on either side (so there are no gaps in the circle other than between the players' legs).
- A football is thrown into the middle.
- Players bend forward and protect their own 'goal' (i.e. the gap between their legs) with their hands.
- Players must try to get others in the circle out by scoring a goal through their legs.
- When a player doesn't defend their goal, and a ball passes through their legs, they first lose a hand. When it happens again, they have to turn around (so they are facing backwards). The third goal that they let in, they are out of the game and leave the circle.
- The game finishes when there are two players left. Have them face back-to-back and start taking steps away from each other. On your command, they turn around, take a deep breath and say 'goal, goal, goal, etc.' on repeat. The first to take a breath loses, and the other wins.

LEGGOALS

Campground FLOOD

This is another ongoing game that you can play throughout your camping trip. Part of the fun is playing it when players aren't expecting it and in different locations.

Number of players: minimum 2, maximum 20
Equipment needed: none
Style of game: mildly active

• Choose a person who is 'on'. They can shout 'flood' whenever they choose and begin counting back from 10.
• When they reach 0, all other players must not be touching the ground (e.g., they could be standing on a tree stump or sitting in a camping chair with their legs in the air).
• Anyone who is not off the ground in time is caught in the flood and is the next person 'on'.
• You can keep playing the game in different places to keep it interesting, or you can make it more of a challenge by saying that you can't use the same place twice (e.g., if you stood on a tree stump to save yourself from the flood, then you can't use it again).

Fifteen Passes provides a more competitive version of simply playing throw and catch. It's easy to pick up and can provide hours of play.

Number of players: minimum 4, maximum 10
Equipment needed: ball
Style of game: active

- Split your group into 2 teams. You may want one team to wear something so you can distinguish between teams during play (such as one team wearing hats).
- Team members must pass the ball to members of their own team without the ball hitting the floor or being blocked.
- When you have the ball, your feet are not allowed to move. Players can block a ball being passed, but can't grab it from someone's hands or physically touch the person holding it.
- The first team to pass 15 times without disruption wins.
- You may want to have a designated area for play, but this isn't necessary.
- If you need to make the game easier or harder, just change the number of passes needed for a team to win.

FIFTEEN PASSES

Categories 

This game works well in the evening. I like to make things extra competitive, so I always have prizes up for grabs for the winning team (or forfeits for the losing team).

Number of players: minimum 7, no maximum
Equipment needed: pen and paper
Style of game: sitting

• Split everyone into small teams of 3-8. You can have as many teams as you like playing against each other.
• Each team is given a piece of paper with a list of chosen categories along the top and a space to put the letters and answers. Ideas for categories include camping gear, Boys' or girls' names, countries, animals, fruits, school subjects, kitchen utensils, famous people, etc. It is even better if you can think of categories that are relevant to your group (ie, teachers' names if you all went to the same school).
• At the start of each round, give the teams a letter - for example, the letter T. Give them 1 minute to decide on a word for each category, beginning with your chosen letter.
• For each correct answer, they get 5 points. If another team has the same answer, though, it goes down to just 1 point. So, thinking of unique words is key.
• Play another round with a new letter.
• When you sense the group is tiring, make that letter the final round before tallying scores.

Screaming Shoes

A quick and enjoyable circle game - it's a game of luck, but players always really get into it!

Number of players: minimum 8, no maximum
Equipment needed: a coin
Style of game: sitting

• Everyone stands in a circle, and all focus on one person's shoes (it doesn't matter who)
• The leader will count to three. On three, everyone must look up and choose one person in the group to look at.
• If the person they have chosen also chooses to look at them (they catch the eyes of each other), then they must scream and sit out. If the person is looking at someone else, then they are fine.
• It is possible to be left with one winner, but at the same time, everyone can be out in one go!

WORD HALT

A laid-back game to play on a lazy morning or while relaxing around the campfire.

Number of players: minimum 4, maximum 16
Equipment needed: pen and paper
Style of game: sitting

- Fold slips of phrases, famous people, names of books or films into a beanie hat and mix them up. Split your players into 2 teams. Pick a slip and show 1 player on each team.
- Choose one of the players and ask them how many words they need in order to describe what is on the slip to their team. The other player can then either choose a lower number if they think they can do it in fewer words, or can say 'I challenge you'. Continue in this way until someone is challenged.
- That player must then attempt to explain what's on the slip with their allocated number of words.
- If their team guesses correctly, then they get a point; if not, the other team gets a point. The team can only collectively have one guess.
- Pick new players and repeat with a different slip.
- The team with the most points at the end of the game wins.

GAMES FOR COUPLES

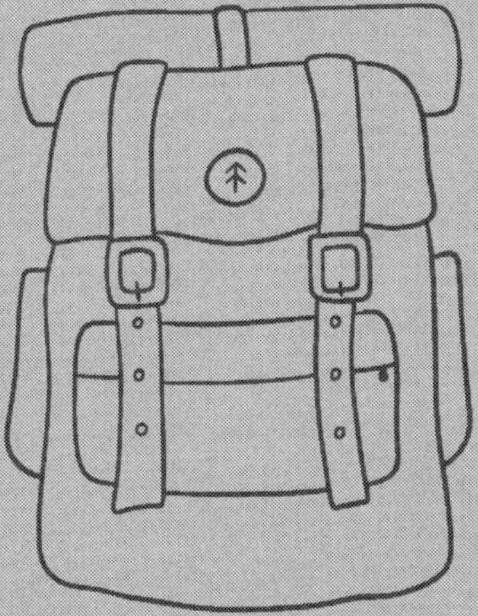

JUST A MINUTE

A swift game that can be played anywhere.

Equipment needed: something to mark 1 minute (i.e., watch or stopwatch on your phone)
Style of game: sitting

- You and your partner take turns playing it.
- The person not playing will be holding the timer and will be in charge of marking out 1 minute.
- The person playing has to choose a topic and talk for a full minute on that topic without hesitation, repeating themselves or switching topics. If any of these things happen, they are out.
- Keep alternating, picking a new topic each time until one of you is out. Or you can play the best of 3.
- If a minute is too difficult, you can compete to see who can speak for the longest on their topic instead.

Let's Go Camping

Let's Go Camping makes a nice little game to kick-start your evening.

Equipment needed: *none*
Style of game: *sitting*

- *One person is chosen to be the Guesser. The other person needs to think of a place to go camping. It needs to be somewhere obscure that you wouldn't usually go camping (a hospital, on a football pitch or in an aeroplane, for example).*
- *The Guesser should make guesses on items they might bring to help them work out where they are going camping (i.e., if it's a hospital, you might pack a mask and prescription, but you wouldn't need a sports kit or a warm blanket)*
- *Once they've guessed correctly, switch roles and start a new game.*

Newlyweds Go Camping

This is a good game to test your relationship. Although it's designed for romantic couples, it can definitely be played by friends (as long as you know each other fairly well). The game requires you to prepare questions in advance, and I recommend doing this before your camping trip.

Equipment needed: pen and paper
Style of game: sitting

- Ahead of the game, write a list of questions to ask each other (you can use the suggestions on the following page or come up with your own). I suggest a mix of easy questions and some slightly more challenging ones.
- Take turns asking each other the questions, at which point both of you write down your answers in secret.
- Once you've written down all your questions, go through the answers together, giving yourselves a point for each answer you both guess correctly.

Example questions:

- *Who is better at putting up a tent?*
- *Who is the funniest?*
- *On a mountain climb, who would reach the summit first?*
- *Who is the tidiest?*
- *Who is the best cook?*
- *Which one of you is better at navigating with a map?*
- *What is their favourite film?*
- *What is their dream adventure?*
- *Who is their celebrity crush?*
- *Who is the most organised?*
- *What is their dream job?*
- *Who is more adventurous?*
- *Who is more honest?*
- *Who will win in an eating competition?*
- *Who is better at starting a fire?*
- *What was their first job?*
- *Who is the better listener?*
- *If they needed a lift at 2 am, who would they call?*
- *What is their ideal way to spend a Friday evening?*
- *Who is more likely to end up famous?*
- *In a survival situation, who would survive the longest?*

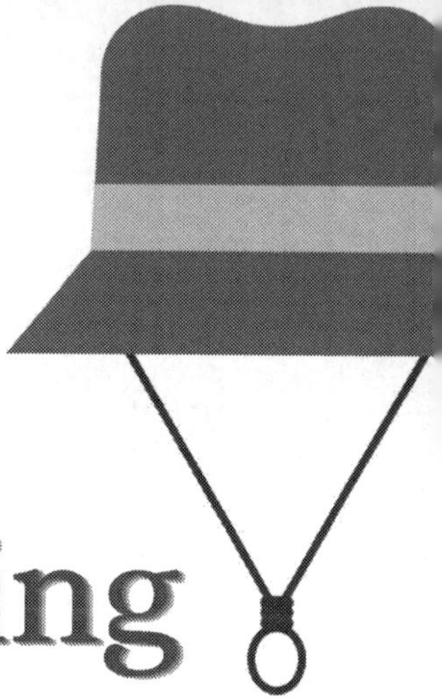

Camping Judo

It's impossible to play this game and not laugh! A rematch (or many) is essential, as the more you play, the better the tactics and moves the players learn, making it all the more fun and competitive.

***Equipment needed**: none*
***Style of game:** mildly active*

- *Two players stand opposite each other, roughly a metre apart.*
- *Each player holds their hands up with their palms facing the other person.*
- *The aim is to make your opponent lose their balance by pushing the other person's hands.*
- *If a player moves their feet or loses balance, then they have lost.*
- *If the games are very short, you can play the best of 3 or add in variations such as playing blindfolded or one-handed.*

For an added challenge, you can play with obstacles in the way (such as trees) or on a hill where the other player is out of sight. As long as you can hear each other shouting your guesses, anything goes!

Equipment needed: none
Style of game: mildly active

• Decide which of the players is the Challenger and which is the Challenged.
• The two players stand back to back and, at a signal (i.e., one of them shouting 'go'), start walking away from each other.
• At some point, as they are walking away from each other, the Challenger yells, 'Halt!' At this point, both players stop and turn around.
• The Challenger must now estimate the smallest number of strides it will take to reach the other.
• When they have given a figure, the Challenged may either give a lower one if they think they can do it in fewer steps, or say, 'Prove it!'.
• If a lower number is given, the bidding continues until one or the other says, 'Prove it!'.
• The player who has been told to prove it must then take strides towards the other, aiming to reach them in the number they estimated or less.
• If they achieve it in the challenged number or less, they have won. If not, then the other player has won.

Halt

KIT LIST MEMORY GAME

Another take on a classic - it translates perfectly to a quick and simple game to play while camping.

Equipment needed: items from your kit
Style of game: sitting

• Select several small items from your kit (start with around 10 items). Lay them out on the floor. Once the position of the items has been decided, they should always return to the same place.
• The player is given 1 minute to memorise the items before closing their eyes or turning around.
• The other player then removes and hides an item from sight. The first player then opens their eyes or turns around and has to guess the item taken.
• Each time they guess an item correctly, a new item is added.
• Players should alternate taking turns.

Riff Off

I like to play this game before bed, often while snuggled up in our sleeping bags.

Equipment needed: none
Style of game: sitting

- One player thinks of a song. They select an important word from that song (i.e., if you choose the song 'My Heart Will Go On', you might select the word 'heart' or 'far' or 'dreams')
- The other player is tasked with trying to get the song.
- If they don't guess it after one word, give them another.
- Keep track of the score (1 point for each word given until the song is correctly guessed).
- The player with the lowest score at the end wins.

This game can be funny or surprisingly heartwarming. I've had some pretty soppy moments with friends and my partner after playing Couple Charades and reminiscing on our shared memories!

Equipment needed: none
Style of game: sitting

• Playing Charades involves one player standing up and acting out something the other player must guess. The player who is acting can't speak, point at things or make noises.
• In Couples Charades, instead of books or movies, you'll choose a memory you share with the person you are playing with, acting out the scene or any other action that may help them guess the memory.
• When the memory is guessed correctly, you swap roles.

COUPLE CHARADES

Other Camping Activity Ideas for Couples

• Go for a night hike, find a place to stop and turn off your torches for 5 minutes to take in the sounds.

• Star gazing (download an app to learn some star constellations)

• Set up blindfold: blindfold one of the couples and task them with setting up camp while the other instructs. You can swap after a while to see who's better at giving instructions and who's better at listening!

• Learn and play a new card game.

• Campfire stories: Task each other to make up a short story to share around the campsite, or simply search and print some from the web to take with you.

• Try Geocaching/Letterboxing together.

• Have a romantic dinner under the stars. Cook an epic camping meal, light the lanterns, lay out the blanket and make your campsite dinner extra special.

CAMPFIRE CHATS

WOULD YOU RATHER?

Would you rather spend a year living in a basic camper van or a luxury glamping tent?

* * *

Would you rather climb a mountain or paddle across a lake?

* * *

Would you rather get up early to see the sunrise or stay up late to see the sunset?

* * *

Would you rather camp on the beach or in the mountains?

* * *

Would you rather be really fast or really strong?

* * *

Would you rather have nonstop rainy weather on a camping trip or be stuck indoors on a beautiful sunny day?

* * *

Would you rather live on a remote island or in the middle of a forest?

* * *

Would you rather spend a year living on a busy tropical island or a remote Scottish island?

* * *

Would you rather hike the length of the Americas or cycle around the world?

Would you rather do a week-long silent retreat in nature or a week-long survival skills course?

* * *

Would you rather wild camp in bear country or in the middle of a desert with no shade?

* * *

Would you rather trek across Patagonia or sail through the Norwegian fjords?

* * *

Would you rather always camp in the cold or always camp in extreme heat?

* * *

Would you rather never get bitten by insects again or never get sunburnt again?

* * *

Would you rather get caught in a hailstorm or in a sandstorm while hiking?

* * *

Would you rather spend a year travelling with a partner or six months solo with double the budget?

* * *

Would you rather live one year completely off-grid or spend a year travelling but always be online?

* * *

Would you rather always have to camp near loud neighbours or never find a flat spot to pitch your tent?

* * *

Would you rather swim in a wild lake or soak in a natural hot spring?

* * *

Would you rather walk the entire length of the UK or canoe the length of the Amazon?

Would you rather climb Mount Everest or row across the Atlantic Ocean?

* * *

Would you rather sleep under the stars with no tent or in a tent during a thunderstorm?

* * *

Would you rather lose your map on a remote trail or your phone in a foreign city?

* * *

Would you rather hike for 12 hours with blisters or sleep one night without a sleeping bag in the cold?

* * *

Would you rather have to forage all your own food for a week or build your own shelter from scratch?

* * *

Would you rather camp with a group of strangers or solo in a remote location?

* * *

Would you rather see the Northern Lights or go on a safari in Africa?

* * *

Would you rather only travel by foot for a year or never be able to walk more than 1 km at a time for a year?

* * *

Would you rather never be able to use a camera again or never be able to use maps/GPS?

* * *

Would you rather have to pack ultra-light with no luxuries or carry a heavy pack with all your comforts?

IF YOU COULD...

Camp in a national park for a month, which would you choose?

* * *

Make any dessert over the campfire tonight; what would you want?

* * *

Choose either to camp alone with no one else around or in a crowded campsite; which would you choose?

* * *

Go on an adventure with someone dead; who would you choose, and what would you do?

* * *

Go on an adventure with someone famous; who would you choose, and what would you do?

* * *

Bring only one comfort item with you when stranded on an island; what would you take?

* * *

To be the greatest in the world at any sport, which would you choose?

* * *

Win a 2-week, all-expenses-paid vacation leaving tomorrow; where would you choose to go?

* * *

Do any long-distance hikes in the world; what would you choose?

If you could only eat one camping meal for the rest of your life, what would you choose?

* * *

Swim in any wild body of water in the world; where would you dive in?

* * *

Sleep in any unique outdoor accommodation for one night; what would it be?

* * *

Have any wild animal safely join you for a day's hike; which animal would you choose?

* * *

Watch the sunrise from anywhere on Earth; where would you be?

* * *

If you could teleport to any trailhead right now, where would you start walking?

* * *

Camp in any extreme environment for 48 hours with proper gear; where would you go?

* * *

Hear one story around the campfire from any historical figure; who would you choose?

* * *

If your tent could be set up anywhere tonight, where would you want to sleep?

* * *

Learn survival skills from any fictional character; who would it be and why?

* * *

Go on an adventure with a famous person, who would you choose?

TELL ME ABOUT...

The most beautiful landscape you've ever seen.

* * *

A time when everything went wrong, but you had fun anyway.

* * *

A person who helped you in a way they may never know.

* * *

The longest hike you've ever done.

* * *

A time you laughed until you cried.

* * *

Your most memorable camping trip.

* * *

A place you went that completely exceeded your expectations.

* * *

A time you failed but it turned out to be a good thing.

A time when you truly stepped out of your comfort zone.

* * *

The scariest moment you've ever had.

* * *

The worst injury you ever sustained.

* * *

The biggest adventure you've ever been on.

A conversation you'll never forget.

* * *

Your favourite childhood vacation.

* * *

A time when you got lost.

* * *

A piece of advice that has always stuck with you.

* * *

The most breathtaking sunrise or sunset you've witnessed.

* * *

Your biggest dream in life.

* * *

Your favourite bit of camping gear.

* * *

A decision that changed the direction of your life.

* * *

A moment when you surprised yourself.

* * *

The most extreme weather you've experienced.

* * *

A risk you took that paid off.

* * *

An unexpected encounter with wildlife.

* * *

A time when you've felt most content.

* * *

The worst night camping you've ever had.

* * *

The first time you went camping on your own.

* * *

A goal you worked really hard to achieve.

CAMPGROUND CHALLENGES

QUICK CHALLENGES, GAMES AND TRICKS

TOFFEE TWIN

Each member of your group picks out the name of another member. The person they pull out of the hat is their Toffee Twin, and they must keep it secret. Once a day, each member must do something nice for their Toffee Twin while keeping their identity a secret.

BANG, BANG, BANG,

The leader holds a finger gun and goes, "Bang, bang, bang, etc," randomly shooting people in the circle. They then ask, "Who's dead?". Everyone has to try to guess who has been shot. Secret: The first person who speaks is the person who dies! See how long it takes them to work out the secret.

* * *

ROPE TANGLE

Tie the wool in a knot so it makes a hoop. Everyone has to hold hands in a circle. The hoop must be passed around the circle without anyone letting go. They must not use fingers, and if they let go, they must start again.

FRUIT CHARADES

Take it in turns to do an impression of a fruit or vegetable without using words, and the others guess.

STICKS CHALLENGE

Get 2 people to balance a stick between their index fingers and walk to a tree and back without it falling. Repeat with four people. Then try with elbows!

UNSTABLE FLOOR

Get a participant to lie flat on the floor, on their belly, hands out straight above their head. Holding their arms, lift the top half of their body off the floor. It is important to tell them to keep their head floppy and drooped to the floor. After a minute, slowly lower them down; they still have to keep their head floppy. When their head touches the floor and their arms keep going, it feels to them like their hands are going through the floor.

CLIMB THROUGH PAPER

Hand over a piece of A4 paper and challenge the person to climb through it. They are allowed to cut it (it's possible....find the solution at the end of the Riddle Answers at the back of the book)

MAKING A KNOT

Hold a piece of rope at both ends. Without letting go, challenge your team to make a knot. Secret: To cross your arms and then pick up the rope. When you uncross your arms, it will make a knot.

DON'T SAY YES

Choose someone to be on. Everyone else must try to get the player to say the word yes. If they say yes, then the person who got them to say it is now on.

PICK UP

Choose a participant and put a long stick (such as a broom) behind their knees (they have to crouch to hold it in place) and also in front of their elbows. Place an object on the floor. The challenge is for them to pick up the object without dropping the stick.

*

COIN TRICK

Press a coin into the middle of your forehead until it sticks there. Then lean your head forward, and tap the back of your head until the coin falls into your hand (can be done easily with practice). Now, ask a participant if they would like to try it. Press the coin into their forehead, but sneakily remove the coin. They will think it is still there and will probably spend a good amount of time hitting the back of their head.

GIANT PICK UP STICKS

Collect sticks that are thin, mostly straight and about a foot in length. To begin, the first player holds all the sticks vertically, making sure that one end is touching the ground. The player quickly releases their hands to let the sticks scatter. Each player then takes it in turns to remove a stick. If any of the sticks move other than the one you have chosen to try and move, then the player loses their go, and it is the next player's turn. The winner is the person who has the most sticks at the end of the game when all of the sticks have been picked up.

BIRTHDAY ORDER

The whole group must order themselves by when their birthday is - January-December - but they cannot talk.

60 SECOND CHALLENGE

The whole group has to stand up. Players sit down when they think a minute has passed. The referee times them, and the winner is the closest to 60 seconds.

FINGER AIKIDO

Players hold each other in a hand-to-hand grip with index fingers pointing out at the other person. The aim is to score points by touching the other player with your index finger. Any part can be touched except the forearm of the hand being used. Players can move around wherever during the game, but they cannot let go of the grip or try to interfere with the other player in any other way.

2 TRUTHS AND A LIE

Everyone is asked to tell the group three things about themselves, either past or present. Two must be true and one is false. The rest of the group must decide which fact they think is false. If you play it again, you can do pet peeves and dislikes or the most bizarre situations you've ever been in.

SCISSORS

Pass two sticks around a circle and say whether they are crossed or uncrossed. The leader says whether the person has it right or wrong. To confuse them, move the sticks around. Secret: If the person's legs are crossed and they say uncrossed, then they are wrong and vice versa.

TABOO

A player is given a card with a word on it —it may be the name of a person, an object, a place, etc. The card will also contain five or six other words that are taboo and cannot be said. The player has to describe, using words alone, what is on their card without using any of the taboo words. The first person to guess what it is becomes the next person to be given a card.

FINGER CIRCLES

Challenge anyone to point their two index fingers towards each other. Start one finger rotating in a circle clockwise. Now, get the other finger rotating anticlockwise. It is impossible!

SILENT PICTURES

An artist is chosen from your group. Using the internet or photos on their phone, they select an image. They return to their group and have 5 minutes to silently convey to their team the image using gestures alone. The person in the group who has the most accurate plcture wins and becomes the next artist.

STACKING CUPS

Place on a table a long piece of string and three plastic cups. The task is to stack the cups using the string without touching the cups at any point. Secret: Make a loop around the cup with the string and twist it in opposite directions until it is tight around the cup. You can then lift and stack the cup and untwist it to release it.

CLOTHES OBSERVATION

Tell your group they are playing a memory game, and ask them to sit in pairs opposite each other. Each pair is given 1 minute to talk about a chosen topic (this is a distraction technique).

Ask each player to then turn around so they can't see each other, and ask them to write down different things about what the other person was wearing – what they had on their feet, what colour their trousers were, etc. At the end, they should face each other and read what they have written to see who has the best memory.

DR TANGLE

Ask your group to stand in a circle facing each other. Everyone puts out their right hand and grabs the hand of someone on their team. Everyone then puts out their left hand and grabs the hand of a different person. Then, ask them to untangle themselves without letting go of each other's hands. If you play it for a second time, you can give them an extra challenge by not talking.

PASS THE GLASS

Get your group to stand in a line, blindfolded. Pass the first person a very full glass of water and get them to pass it along the line without spilling any. You can make the game harder by having an obstacle course and splitting into 2 teams to complete the course. The team with the fullest glass at the end wins.

AFTER EIGHT CHALLENGE

Everyone has to place an after-eight on their forehead. The aim is to be the first to eat the after eight without using their hands. It can also be played with a cookie or a chocolate-covered biscuit.

DRAWING

Hold up a stick and draw a moon in the air. Then, pass it around the circle and tell everyone to copy you. If they say thank you when the stick is passed to them, then they are right; if not, then they are wrong.

RIGHT HAND CHALLENGE

Simply ask everyone to put their right hand where their left hand can't reach. Secret: Put it on your left elbow.

CAMPFIRE RIDDLES

1. If I drink it, I die. If I eat it, I die. A blind man sees it. A deaf man hears it. What am I?

* * *

2. Victoria and David Beckham are lying dead on the floor; there is glass and water everywhere. What happened?

* * *

3. What is the beginning of eternity, the end of time and space, the beginning of every end and the end of every place?

* * *

4. I live in the kitchen. I am round and deep. But I can never be filled. What am I?

* * *

5. I can't be touched, but I can touch you. I can take you far away, but I don't move. What am I?

* * *

6. I end in a W, yet I have no end. What am I?

* * *

7. I am a cheese that is made in reverse. What am I?

* * *

8. A five-letter word that is the same when read the right way up and upside down?

* * *

9. The more you remove, the larger I become. What am I?

10. If you write every number between 50 and 100, how many times would you write the number 7?

* * *

11. What has a bottom at the top?

* * *

12. A child says her age in 2 years time will be twice the age she was 5 years ago. How old is the child now?

* * *

13. There is a square room with eight monkeys in it. There are two monkeys in one corner, two in the next, two in the next and two in the last, how many monkeys can say they can see another monkey?

* * *

14. I have rivers but no water, Forests with no trees, Mountains but no rocks and towns without buildings. What am I?

* * *

15. What goes up and down stairs without moving?

* * *

16. I have a head and a tail but no body. What am I?

* * *

17. There's none in a day. There are two in a week. There's one in a year. What am I?

* * *

18. When you say my name, I am lost. What am I?

* * *

19. I am a token of love. I have no beginning and no end. What am I?

* * *

20. Whoever makes me sells me. Whoever buys me doesn't need me. Whoever needs me doesn't buy me. What am I?

21. The more you take of me, the more you leave behind. What am I?

* * *

22. I'm always coming but never come. What am I?

* * *

23. There is a pole in the middle of a field and a donkey attached to a 10-metre piece of rope. A bucket of water is 11 metres away from the pole. How does the donkey drink from the bucket?

* * *

24. A plane crashes on the border of France and Germany. Where do you bury the 24 survivors?

* * *

25. A man is driving down a long road with trees on either side of him. There is no moonlight, stars, headlights, streetlights, or cats' eyes. A black cat runs in front of the car, and the man swerves. How does the man see the cat?

* * *

26. Someone at a party introduces you to your mother's only sister's husband's sister-in-law. He has no brothers. What do you call this lady?

* * *

27. A carpenter was in a terrible hurry. He had to work as quickly as possible to cut a very heavy 10-foot plank into 10 equal sections. If it takes one minute per cut, how long will it take him to get the 10 equal pieces?

* * *

28. What English word can have 4 of its 5 letters removed and still retain its original pronunciation?

* * *

29. Johnny's mother had three children. The first child was named April, and the second child was named May. What was the third child's name?

30. A woman goes into a hardware store to buy something for her house. When asked the price, the clerk replies, "The price of one is twelve cents, the price of forty-four is twenty-four cents, and the price of a hundred and forty-four is thirty-six cents. What does the woman want to buy?

* * *

31. What question may be asked of you? But the reply will never be yes.

* * *

32. If there are 5 apples on the counter and you take away 2, how many do you have?

* * *

33. If having only one match, on a freezing winter's day, you entered a room containing a lamp, a kerosene heater, and a wood-burning stove, which should you light first?

* * *

34. There is a light in a room and 3 light switches outside the room. Once you've gone into the room, you can't come back out again. How do you work out which light switch turns on the light?

* * *

35. I'm a bus driver and the other day I was driving a route. At the first stop, 7people got on the bus, at the second stop it 13 people got on and three gotoff. At the final stop, 4 people got on, and 7 people got off. What's the name of the bus driver?

* * *

36. Charles was racing around in his new sports car when he noticed that his throat was parched. He came to a screeching halt in front of a public house, and the nine police cars which had been chasing him slammed into the back of his car and each other's. How many bumpers will have been hit?

37. When Sandy was six years old she hammered a nail into her favourite tree to mark her height. Ten years later at sweet sixteen Sandy returned to see how much higher the nail was. If the tree grew by five centimetres each year, how much higher would the nail be?

* * *

38. I throw a ball, and it completely stops, changes direction, and comes back again; how?

* * *

39. I go to town on Friday, stay one night in a hotel and leave the next day on Friday. How?

Answers at the end of the book!

A NOTE FROM BEX BAND....

Thank you for picking up a copy of Camping Games for Adults!

This book was a labour of love. I collected years' worth of games and activities and tested them out on family and friends.

It was a lot of fun creating this book, but it wasn't always easy. As any parent will know, it's a serious juggle managing any passion project alongside looking after small humans. But the juggle is always worth it when pursuing your dreams!

I have a small (but important!) favour to ask. As a teeny-tiny independent author, one of the biggest factors in how successful my book will be is the number of reviews I have.

I'd therefore be incredibly grateful if you could take a minute **right now** to head to Amazon and leave a short review. I know you are busy and have a million things to do, so I want to say the biggest thank you to anyone who does this.

Remember also to find me on social media (@Bex_Band) and feel free to get in touch via my website www.bexband.com. I love hearing from readers.

Before we part ways, I'd also like to share with you the opening chapter of my bestselling and award-winning memoir, *Three Stripes South*. If you like the outdoors, I think this is a story you might enjoy......

The opening chapter from Bex Band's memoir, Three Stripes South. The 1000km hike that changed everything....

Winner
SHEXTREME BOOK AWARD

Shortlisted
TGO OUTDOOR BOOK of the **YEAR**

Chapter 1

Is there anything more reliable in life than a toilet cubicle? Locked in a familiar cocoon of white walls, knowing this space is, temporarily, only for you, you are offered a few moments of uninterrupted peace to do as you please. You can simply sit there looking dishevelled without needing to care, give yourself the headspace to conjure up an internal pep talk or waste time on your phone away from judgemental stares.

It was in a toilet cubicle that I found myself trying to calm my nerves after a noisy flight and the chaotic mayhem that is Israeli airport arrivals. I'd had to answer a dozen questions on who I was and where I'd come from to get through. When I eventually received the stamp of approval, saying that I was granted entry, my stress levels increased even more. The reason for my being in the country suddenly felt very real and I had the overwhelming feeling I was spinning downhill out of control, past the point of being able to slam on the brakes.

Usually, arriving in a foreign airport is accompanied by excitement as you anticipate all the joyous fun that lies ahead on your holiday. This was different, though. I'd gone to Israel not to spend time on a beach or to explore the many sites of the Holy Land, but to take on the biggest, most daunting challenge of my life – and I was seriously starting to question if I'd made a terrible mistake.

A flight announcement on the overhead speakers brought me back to reality and the white walls of the cubicle. I left the safety of the toilets to rejoin Gil who was waiting outside with our luggage, checking his phone for the umpteenth time since landing. My husband was anxious for an altogether different reason. His parents had made the three-hour round trip from their home town to come meet us off the plane at Tel Aviv and it wasn't fair for me to keep him from them any longer.

I heard the squeal of excitement from my mother-in-law as we turned the final corner of the airport maze, hitting a wall of waiting loved ones and taxi drivers. Mira and Amir stood among them, their smiles beaming. There were hugs, more squealing and then more hugs. Amir, my father-in-law, took my face in his large hands, forcing me to look at him, then gently slapped my cheek twice in a gesture that made me think of *The Godfather*. I'd like to say that this effusive welcome was because it had been so long since we'd last seen them, but Israeli greetings, especially in Gil's family, were drawn-out and affectionate even if you were just returning from an hour's trip to the supermarket.

Amir bent down, picked up my large rucksack and threw it over his broad shoulder with ease, before making his way towards the exit.

'You are really doing this hike, then?' he said in his gruff voice, thick with accent. It was exactly the question I'd been asking myself on repeat throughout the entire flight. Was I really going to do this hike?

Of course, the border control officer, with her mass of curly hair unsuccessfully tied back in a bun, had wanted to know why I was visiting Israel. I'd thought about making up a lie, thinking my real reason might seem too far-fetched, but concluded that this was definitely not the place to be trying to distort the truth. Israeli border control was ruthless and unforgiving.

'I'm walking the Israel National Trail,' I'd told her with forced conviction.

Chapter 1

She looked up from my passport, one eyebrow raised. 'The whole thing?'

'Yes.'

'Really?'

'Yes,' I insisted, shifting from one leg to the other. While I'd been making my plans and talking to people about walking the 1,020-kilometre Israel National Trail for months now, I realised that this border control officer was one of the few people I'd said it out loud to who had actually heard of the trail, and who knew the scale of the challenge that Gil and I had signed up for.

'How long will it take?'

'About eight weeks in total.'

She looked back at my passport, at her computer screen, then held my gaze, looking at me for more than was comfortable. I stood still and tried hard to ignore my instinct to glance away or smile, worried that my nerves would make it seem as though I was lying. After what felt like a really long time, she leant over and grabbed a stamp, slamming it down hard.

'Good luck,' she said, my passport slung casually between her fingers as she handed it back, already looking past me at the next person in line. 'You'll need it. It's hot.'

Hot it was. Stepping out of the cool, air-conditioned airport, we walked into a wall of heat. I took a deep breath. The dusty air and heavy humidity was suffocating, making my lungs feel like they needed to work that extra bit harder just to get enough oxygen in. Amir's hand, which was still softly holding the back of my neck and guiding me forward, gave a squeeze. He was waiting for an answer.

'Yep. I guess so, Amir. We're really doing this hike.'

* * * *

I'd first heard of the Israel National Trail while sitting at my desk, scrolling through social media, having just taken a bite of my Marmite sandwich. I was coming to the end of a year of teacher training and, just like in all my previous jobs, break times were my favourite part of the day. I often used them to escape in the maze of the internet, daydreaming, being nosy and making plans for my weekends and time off.

The usual content whizzed past me on the screen, updates from friends, adverts and interesting articles shared, when a word caught my eye, *Adventure*. It was part of a heading that led me to an article about the best hikes in the world, and that's where I saw it for the first time: the Israel National Trail.

I immediately left the article to do a search so I could find out more, landing on the official page for the trail. The Israel National Trail is a hike stretching the full length of the country, from the Israel-Lebanon border to Eilat on the Gulf of Aqaba. It passes mountains in the north, follows the coastline to Tel Aviv and heads through thick forests near Jerusalem before cutting straight across the Negev, a huge desert which covers more than half of the country.

There were other hikes featured in the article but this one immediately stood out because of my ties to the country. Israel had never been on my radar, but then neither had meeting a future husband, certainly not one from a different country. I had been by Lake Atitlán in Guatemala travelling and learning Spanish, shortly after finishing university. It just so happened that the week I joined the Spanish school there was only one other beginner starting at the same time. I met Gil in the afternoon Conversation Club after our one-to-one lessons had finished. Fresh from his mandatory army service, tanned, with dark features, he oozed endless optimism and was enjoying life in the way that only a 22-year-old can. It didn't take me long to fall completely in love. In fact, it was just a week later that I found myself in an internet café on a phone call with my mum declaring I had met the man I wanted to marry.

'A Guatemalan?!' she said excitedly.

'Uh, no. Actually he's Israeli.'

'OK. Well, make sure you're being safe.' My mum took my hopeful declaration of marriage in her stride, as I knew she would. She told me to just enjoy myself, although I picked up on a hint of scepticism about the situation. I felt it too. A girl from Basingstoke and a boy from Israel meeting in a Spanish school in Guatemala, although romantic, would surely never work out.

Just four months later, though, and Gil was on a plane to the UK to start a new life with me in London, a city that was new for both of us. Despite there being a fresh coating of snow on the ground outside, he walked out of the terminal wearing nothing more than shorts, sandals and a knitted jumper he'd picked up in a market in Central America. First stop was a shopping mall, where I bought him a late Hanukkah present: a coat and a pair of woolly socks.

The very existence of long-distance trails was a completely new discovery for me. It amazed me that there were people out there that did these sorts of things, real-life adventurers. I was finding out that our country had things like national parks and mountain ranges, environments that were alien to me. I began devouring books, magazines, films and talks by adventurers, fascinated by it all. Time and again I heard the same message: 'If I can do this, you can too; anything is possible if you put your mind to it'. I heard this from people who had climbed Everest, or rowed an ocean or cycled around the world. Hugely expensive, physically demanding feats that were so far removed from what I knew. Almost all the adventurers I saw fitted one type of mould. White men who oozed the distinct and unshakable confidence instilled by a public-school upbringing. They wore bushy beards and displayed cabinets filled with evidence of sporting achievements and awards they'd collected in their younger years. They had a need to conquer, claiming world firsts and record-breaking feats. I was far from fitting in to the world of adventure. Unfit and inexperienced in the outdoors, I hated regular exercise, trauma from my overweight days and humiliating PE classes never quite having left me. I'd collected far more detentions in my school years than awards. I wasn't a hiker or a camper and didn't know how to navigate using a map and, worse still, I didn't even have any outdoorsy friends or family that I could ask for advice.

The Israel National Trail would be a huge undertaking, something that felt scary and beyond me, but still, I was drawn to it and, even more, to the emotions it stirred up inside me when I imagined standing on the trail, a large bag on my back and a dramatic landscape up ahead. The truth was I was feeling like a failure at life, like nothing I started came to completion, like, no matter how hard I tried, I couldn't quite find solid ground. While friends around me began climbing their way up successful careers and putting down deposits on shiny new builds, I was struggling to find the motivation to even get out of bed most days. I knew I needed a change and perhaps this hike would be it. A challenge and a chance to prove myself.

The decision to do the hike, taken just like that, still chewing on the last bites of my Marmite sandwich, would send me sprinting down a new path in life. It was a fleeting moment, a chance discovery and a brave decision, but first there was a tiny obstacle: I would need to let my husband know that he would be joining me. If this was going to happen, if I was really going to dismantle our lives to take on this obscure challenge, we'd need to be in it together.

* * * *

I watched Gil take off his suit and slip into more comfortable clothes. The lounge and bedroom shared the same space in our split-level Putney studio. I saw his demeanour change as it did every night, the stresses and strains of his busy City job stripping away as the tie came off, slung over a clothes hanger, ready for the next morning. He joined me on the sofa and looked at me expectantly, sensing I had something to say. I shifted in my seat.

'You know I'm not very happy at the moment?'

Gil nodded, gently taking my hand in his.

'I need a change. I think we both need a change, actually.'

When we first moved to London, five years earlier, we made a list of a hundred things we wanted to do in the city. It was a time of playful fun, imagining all the places we would visit. On weekends we'd head out into the centre to see museums, take boat tours along the Thames, watch shows or take selfies in front of landmarks. There had been some more out-there ideas thrown in the mix as well. One day we'd thrown away our inhibitions to join a flash mob and on another occasion we managed to blag our way behind the scenes of a Rolling Stones concert in Hyde Park. With just twenty things left to go, though, the list had been left tacked on our wardrobe untouched for almost two years. Something had shifted. Absorbed as we were in work, chasing promised promotions and an ever-growing pile of paperwork, free time now felt like a luxury reserved only for catching up with sleep, food shopping and laundry, not for having fun.

'I think we should both leave our jobs and hike the Israel National Trail.'

Gil's eyebrows shot up. Although his family had exposed him to things like day hiking and camping, you were more likely to find him in his youth in the lighting box in a drama hall than on the sports field. He, like me, had slotted in well to the unfit convenience lifestyle of city living and was not someone you would expect to see doing a long-distance hike.

He was now fiddling with the wedding ring on his finger; eight months on, he still couldn't get used to wearing it.

'When do you want to go?'

'I was thinking towards the end of this year. They say it takes about two months to do the whole thing. I can only get a three-month visa to visit the country, so it wouldn't give us a lot of time if we needed a few days beforehand to prepare, but we should be able to manage it.' There are only two safe windows for hiking the Israel National Trail, one in spring and one in autumn. The desert is a dangerous place to be in summer, when the temperatures soar, and in winter, when the risk of flash flooding is at its highest. Although it was only February, I knew spring would be too soon to get everything ready and to have saved up the money we would need to complete the hike, which made autumn our next window of opportunity.

'But I'd miss my end-of-year bonus.'

Not just the bonus, I thought, knowing there would be a lot more sacrifices made. 'You would. But we've been saying for ages that we want to go away. There's always going to be a reason not to do it. I just feel like… it just feels like we should…' I tailed off, not sure how to explain how it just felt right in my gut, even if every rational thought was telling me it was wrong, that doing the hike didn't make any sense at all.

'And our jobs?'

'I'll have finished my teacher training by then, so could probably just pick up a teaching job when I get back. And maybe you could ask for a sabbatical.' We both knew Gil's job would never approve one. Agreeing to this hike would mean saying goodbye to the job he had worked so hard to get, along with the promotion that his manager had been hinting at. We would be losing our financial security and savings. I also wasn't sure how easy it would be to get a teaching job after taking a break straight after completing my training. There would be a lot of uncertainty hanging over our return.

He sighed and looked out of the window at the Tube crossing Putney Bridge, the train windows steamed up from the squashed commuters inside who were lit up against the drab, dark winter sky. 'Don't the trains passing by bother you?' guests would always ask when they felt the flat shake like a mild earthquake every few minutes. They never did. I didn't even notice the shaking anymore.

Gil turned back to me. 'The Israel National Trail,' he said, as if playing with the words out loud, before a slight grin appeared in the corner of his mouth. 'I'm in. Let's do it.'

The next day we booked our flights. It felt like the signature at the end of a contract, the seal of an envelope. We had cemented our decision.

Could it really be that easy? The hike felt like such a momentous thing, but the hardest part of getting to the start had been the simple act of just saying yes.

What followed was a methodical taking apart of our lives, chipping away at a to-do list one task after another. With the click of an email, we left the careers we had spent years working towards. We decluttered and reduced our possessions and handed in the notice on our flat. We moved in with family for our final weeks and had our goodbye parties with friends. All my spare time was now reserved for searching the internet desperately looking for answers to all the things I didn't know: 'How hard is it to hike one thousand kilometres?' 'How do you go to the toilet outdoors?' 'What animals can kill you in the desert?'

Finally, all that was left was our boarding passes and two bulky backpacks that sat in the corner of our temporary bedroom. Looking at all the shiny and perfectly organised gear, I couldn't decide if it made me feel more prepared and ready for the trail or more like I was well and truly out of my depth. Either way, and despite all the nerves and doubting, the presence of the packs made me certain of one thing. It felt good to be doing something different, taking a proactive step, shaking up our lives.

Maybe this would turn out to be a good decision or maybe it wouldn't. One thing was certain, though. This was going to be an adventure.

Other books by Bex Band....

RIDDLE ANSWERS

1. Nothing
2. They are fish whose bowl fell on the floor
3. The letter E
4. A sieve
5. A Story
6. A Rainbow
7. Edam
8. SWIMS
9. A hole
10. 15
11. A leg!
12. 12
13. None...monkeys can't talk!
14. A map
15. A carpet
16. A coin
17. Letter E
18. Silence
19. A Ring
20. A Coffin
21. Footsteps
22. Tomorrow
23. The donkey isn't attached to the pole.
24. You don't bury them. They're survivors.
25. It is the middle of the day
26. Mother
27. 9 minutes
28. Queue
29. Johnny

30. House numbers
31. Are you asleep?
32. 2
33. The match
34. You turn switch I on for 5 minutes, then off. Then turn switch 2 on and go into the room. If the bulb is off and warm, it's switch 1. If it's off and cold, then it's switch 3. If it's on, then it's switch 2.
35. The person who is telling the riddle.
36. Since ten cars are involved, all the bumpers will have been hit except the front one on Charles's car and the back one on the last police car.
37. The nail would be at the same height since trees grow at their tops.
38. I throw it up.
39. Friday is the name of a horse.

CLIMB THROUGH PAPER SOLUTION

You need to cut the paper like this:

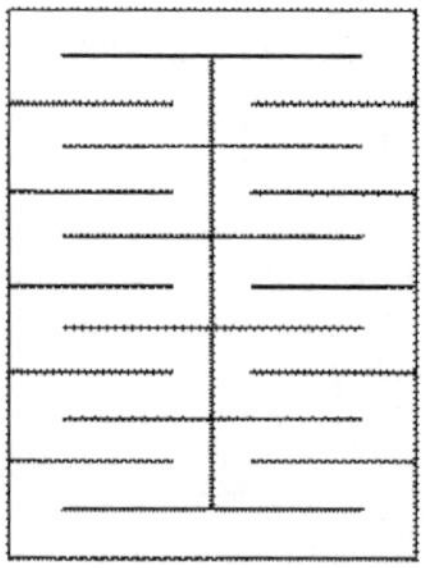

Made in the USA
Las Vegas, NV
28 April 2026

46062499R00059